Legal Support to Operations

Air Force Doctrine Document 1-04

4 March 2012

This document complements related discussion found in Joint Publication 1-04, *Legal Support to Military Operations*.

BY ORDER OF THE
SECRETARY OF THE AIR FORCE

AIR FORCE DOCTRINE DOCUMENT 1-04
4 MARCH 2012

SUMMARY OF CHANGES

This revision restructures the entire publication for better presentation of key ideas. The publication's title changed to better align with legal support provided to the commander, Air Force forces (COMAFFOR). This AFDD discusses the Judge Advocate General and command fundamentals (Chapter One); expands discussion on the command and organization of Air Force judge advocate general corps personnel support (Chapter Two); and identifies key aspects of judge advocate general support to Air Force operations, to include readiness and planning (Chapter Three).

Supersedes: AFDD 2-4.5, 15 May 2003
OPR: LeMay Center/DDS
Certified by: LeMay Center/DD (Col Todd C. Westhauser)
Pages: 55
Accessibility: Publications are available on the e-publishing website at www.e-publishing.af.mil for downloading
Releasability: There are no releasability restrictions on this publication
Approved by: Thomas K. Andersen, Major General, USAF
              Commander, Curtis E. LeMay Center for Doctrine Development and Education

FOREWORD

Air Force Doctrine Document (AFDD) 1-04, *Legal Support to Operations*, establishes Air Force doctrine focused on legal advice and considerations for Air Force operations. The Air Force, like other Services, continues to operate in an increasingly complex environment around the world, demanding nothing less than the very best in legal capability. This document represents best practices and other sanctioned ideas regarding legal aspects of Air Force operations across the range of military operations. For over 60 years, the Air Force has possessed organic legal support in both the Office of the General Counsel and the Judge Advocate General (JAG) corps. On 25 June 1948, the US Congress established the office of The Judge Advocate General (TJAG), and, a year later, the Air Force Chief of Staff designated Air Force officers—who are attorneys—to serve as JAGs. In 2003, the JAG Department was renamed the "JAG corps" by order of the Secretary of the Air Force.

The Office of the Judge Advocate General (JA) and the Office of the Air Force General Counsel (GC) work together to serve the Department of the Air Force. The relationship between GC and JA is unique. Both the General Counsel and TJAG are legal advisers to the Secretary of the Air Force and Chief of Staff of the Air Force with right of independent access and independent legal advice to those officials. JA and GC work in a complementary manner on a wide variety of issues. As such, this AFDD does not address the roles and responsibilities of GC, issues may arise in the field that fall in areas for which GC is responsible.

Legal support to Air Force commanders is critical to mission success. They turn primarily to their JAGs for insight into the law and its impact on Air Force operations. Proper legal counsel enhances commanders' successful decision-making ability, aiding in mission success.

THOMAS K. ANDERSEN
Major General, USAF
Commander, LeMay Center for Doctrine
Development and Education

TABLE OF CONTENTS

PREFACE

This AFDD focuses on fundamental principles, organization of legal support, and conduct of legal support operations by JAG corps personnel.

Chapter One, *Judge Advocate General and Command Fundamentals*, describes the power of command and fundamental Air Force legal aspects of command. It also details the legal roles and responsibilities of the (COMAFFOR) to include: mission accomplishment, compliance with the law, and maintenance of domestic and foreign contracts.

Chapter Two, *Command and Organization of Air Force JAG Corps Support*, introduces JAG corps organization including: TJAG, the Air Force Legal Operations Agency (AFLOA), and Staff Judge Advocates (SJA). It describes the integration of legal support into the air operations center divisions.

Chapter Three, *JAG Corps Support to Air Force Operations*, describes how the Air Force conducts legal support operations. It discusses legal considerations across the range of military operations, operations planning, Air Force legal readiness, mission readiness of JAG corps personnel, rules of engagement, and rules for the use of force.

Five appendices complement this AFDD by expanding concepts presented within the chapters. These appendices provide additional legal considerations for Air Force operations, deliberate and crisis action planning, legal readiness considerations, rules of engagement, and US code sections.

This document applies to all Airmen.

CHAPTER ONE

JUDGE ADVOCATE GENERAL AND COMMAND FUNDAMENTALS

> *"The High Contracting Parties at all times, and the parties to the conflict in time of armed conflict, shall ensure that legal advisers are available, when necessary, to advise military commanders at the appropriate level on the application of the conventions and this protocol and on the appropriate instruction to be given to the armed forces on this subject."*
>
> **Geneva Additional Protocol I**
> **Article 82**
>
> *Although the US is not a party to Protocol 1, the US considers this to be a good practice.*

This chapter discusses the power of command and fundamental Air Force legal aspects of command. It also details the legal roles and responsibilities of the commander, Air Force forces (COMAFFOR) to include: mission accomplishment, compliance with the law, and maintaining domestic and foreign contracts. Because the COMAFFOR is normally dual-hatted as the joint or combined force air component commander (JFACC/CFACC), "the requirements and responsibilities of the COMAFFOR and JFACC/CFACC are inextricably linked".[1] However, this document is written specifically to inform the Air Force commander about the legal support available to him and will refer to the COMAFFOR, even in instances where that individual is also likely the JFACC/CFACC.

THE POWER OF COMMAND

The COMAFFOR is responsible for ensuring that Air Force forces understand and comply with legal requirements. The COMAFFOR's staff judge advocate (SJA) is responsible for providing timely and effective legal advice to the COMAFFOR. Effective discharge of this responsibility requires commanders to understand their legal responsibilities and the capabilities of an SJA. The commander's legal authority is derived from the Constitution and from statutes enacted by Congress. The legal directives that provide for a commander's authority are only part of the equation.

The power and responsibilities of command are distinctive elements of military operations. How commanders wield this power can determine success or failure of the mission according to the following principles:

---

[1] See AFDD 1.

- Command is the responsibility of an individual, not a staff.

- Command is exercised by virtue of the office and the assignment of officers holding military grades who are eligible by law to command.

- A commander can exercise command authority through subordinate commanders.

- Vice and deputy commanders have no command functions. However, they assist the commander via planning, investigating, and providing recommendations.

- Some command authorities may be delegated; however, the responsibilities of command may never be delegated.

The concept of command embodies two important functions. First, it is the legal authority over people, including the power to discipline. Second, command is the legal responsibility for assigned resources and mission accomplishment.

COMAFFOR LEGAL ROLES AND RESPONSIBILITIES

The role of a commander is unlike any position found in the civilian world, and unlike almost any other found in government. A COMAFFOR not only has the legal authority to perform various roles and responsibilities, but also has the corresponding legal obligation to meet requirements defined by their roles and responsibilities. Accordingly, commanders are accountable for the following:

- Mission accomplishment.

- Compliance with the law, to include:

  - US law.

  - Local or host-nation law, when required.

  - International law, as appropriate.

- Maintaining domestic and foreign contracts (as required for mission accomplishment).

Mission Accomplishment

A COMAFFOR's foremost legal responsibilities are to follow the orders of their superior joint force commander (JFC) and accomplish the assigned mission or task. The COMAFFOR's immediate task is to organize, and when directed, employ an effective fighting force responsive to orders in a disciplined and effective manner.

Compliance with the Law

Public confidence in the military is maintained and strengthened by Airmen, particularly commanders, performing their responsibilities in a manner that is objective, fact-based, non-partisan, and non-ideological. A commander's credibility is based on objectivity in discharging his or her responsibilities. The continued viability of the commander's legal authority, particularly the authority to maintain good order and discipline, depends upon public and US government belief that commanders can be fair and objective. Objectivity includes the perception of independence: Maintaining impartiality, having intellectual honesty, and remaining free of conflicts of interest. Maintaining objectivity includes a continuing assessment of relationships, particularly with private entities, in the context of a commander's responsibility to the public.

United States Law

Every Airman makes a solemn promise to "support and defend the Constitution of the United States against all enemies, foreign and domestic, and bear true faith and allegiance to the same." Commanders bear the burden of ensuring Air Force personnel comply with US law. It is their responsibility to ensure good order and discipline. George Washington once stated, "Discipline is the soul of the Army." The original, and still most important, SJA mission is supporting the commander in administering good order and discipline. Effective command and control of a force can only be exercised if that force maintains good order and discipline.

Local or Host-Nation Law

In many cases, the Air Force is not directly bound by local or host-nation laws. In the US, many state laws do not bind the Air Force since it is a federal entity. In the overseas environment, the Air Force is often not bound by host-nation law due to basing agreements or status of forces agreements (SOFAs) allowing Air Force operations.

It is important for the commander and local authorities to fully understand the extent to which the Air Force is bound by any host-nation law. A further challenge is ensuring individual Airmen comply with host-nation or state law. Whereas the Air Force as an entity may not have to comply, there is a much greater chance that individual Airmen will be expected to comply with local law. Here the commander has a critical role to ensure local authorities are respected to the maximum extent possible, while maintaining fair treatment of Airmen. JAGs provide advice on local and host-nation law. When compliance issues arise, they negotiate with local and state authorities on a commander's behalf.

International Law

International law is a highly complex aspect of international relations that is becoming increasingly important in the context of military operations. Some aspects of international law are well known to the commander, such as the law of armed conflict (LOAC). Others may not be well known, such as the concept of international human rights. JAG training results in a basic understanding of international law. The SJA maintains a group of JAGs who are specially trained to provide advice and support to the commander on applicable international law issues.

Maintaining Domestic and Foreign Contracts

Contracting (with non-military organizations) is often required for mission accomplishment. While there are mechanisms in place for subordinate personnel to work the processes to commission and manage contracts, the contracting officer is primarily responsible for advising the commander on contracting issues. Many contracts between the Air Force and non-military organizations are complex. JAGs can provide the understanding commanders require in the highly regulated realm of contracting relationships (both domestic and foreign). The commander's actual legal authority may not be commensurate with his perceived responsibility to maintain or develop a contract. For accurate understanding of contractual obligations and responsibilities, commanders should consult their JAGs.

CHAPTER TWO

COMMAND AND ORGANIZATION OF JAG CORPS SUPPORT

> **JAG CORPS MISSION**
> *Under the direction of The Judge Advocate General, the JAG Corps delivers professional, candid, independent counsel and full-spectrum legal capabilities to command and the warfighter.*
>
> **JAG CORPS VISION**
> *Enabling the Air Force and the warfighter through mission-focused legal capabilities honed for a dynamic environment.*

This chapter describes the Air Force JAG organizational structure and JAG Corps organization including: The Judge Advocate General (TJAG), the Air Force Legal Operations Agency (AFLOA), and SJA. It describes the integration of legal support into the Air Operations Center (AOC).

JAG CORPS ORGANIZATION

The Judge Advocate General

Under federal law, TJAG is the legal advisor to the Secretary of the Air Force (SECAF), the Chief of Staff of the Air Force (CSAF), and all officers and agencies of the Department of the Air Force. TJAG directs Air Force JAGs and paralegals in the performance of their duties.

Federal law also provides that no officer or employee of the Department of Defense may interfere with:

○ The ability of TJAG to give independent legal advice to the SECAF or CSAF.

○ The ability of JAGs assigned or attached to, or performing duty with, military units to give independent legal advice to commanders.

The Air Force JAG Corps organization includes the following personnel:

○ TJAG and Deputy Judge Advocate General (DJAG).

○ All other Air Force officers designated as JAGs.

○ Airmen in the paralegal services career field and those assigned duties in JAG offices at any level of command.

○ Civilian attorneys and legal services civilians supporting the JAG Corps mission.

✪ Air Force Reserve Component officers designated as JAGs.

✪ Air Force Reserve Component enlisted personnel in the paralegal services career field and those assigned duties in JAG offices at any level of command.

Commanders should note that, despite any temporary duties a JAG may be assigned, they retain their status as a JAG Corps member.

Air Force Legal Operations Agency

AFLOA is a field-operating agency comprised of more than 800 military and civilian attorneys, paralegals, and support personnel worldwide. AFLOA provides TJAG with civil, commercial, and criminal law expertise and litigation support, as well as legal education and cutting-edge technological assets. The divisions of AFLOA, including the JAG School and the JAG corps field support centers (FSCs), provide direct legal services and support throughout the Air Force. The AFLOA commander ensures that FSCs regularly communicate with SJAs to maintain effective lines of communication and ensure support to field commanders.

Staff Judge Advocates

The SJA is the senior JAG assigned to provide legal advice to a court-martial convening authority (the Air Force commander with authority to convene general or special courts-martial). The convening authority is typically exercised by the installation or host unit commander. SJAs also provide legal advice and services to commanders of tenant units served by the host unit. The principal responsibility of the SJA is to provide full-spectrum legal services required by commanders and their staffs.

By law, commanders responsible for convening courts-martial should at all times communicate directly with the SJA in matters relating to the administration of military justice. By law, SJAs are authorized to communicate directly with the SJA of a superior or subordinate command or with TJAG. No officer or employee of the Department of Defense (DOD) may interfere with the ability of JAGs to give independent legal advice.

Field Support Centers

FSCs are TJAG's primary vehicle for providing legal reachback support to field commanders through their SJA and JAG corps. FSCs provide added legal expertise concerning a particular legal issue by coordinating with, and acting through, a commander's SJA. As the commander's single focal point for all legal services, the SJA is solely responsible for identifying when a particular legal issue merits the additional legal expertise an FSC provides. If warranted, an SJA may seek FSC expertise in areas such as aircraft investigations, claims, government contracts, and environmental issues or labor issues.

STAFF JUDGE ADVOCATE TO THE COMAFFOR ORGANIZATION

The COMAFFOR has several staff activities that fulfill specific responsibilities. These activities are usually related to providing close, personal advice or services to the commander, or assisting the commander and the component staff with technical, administrative, or tactical matters. The COMAFFOR's SJA provides the full spectrum of legal services and advice to the COMAFFOR and Air Force forces (AFFOR) staff.

JAGs and paralegals focus on legal issues affecting the COMAFFOR's ability to provide mission-ready air, space, and cyberspace capabilities, such as those relating to the planning; deployment; reception, staging, onward movement and integration; sustainment; and redeployment of forces. With assistance from JAGs and paralegals, the COMAFFOR establishes and maintains good order and discipline for all members assigned or attached to an air expeditionary task force (AETF). The AFFOR SJA provides guidance and managerial oversight to all subordinate JAGs and paralegals.

The AFFOR staff (also called the "A-staff") and the air operations center (AOC) have distinctly separate duties. Therefore, the AFFOR JAG corps personnel should not be dual-hatted as legal advisors to the COMAFFOR and AOC. Ideally, the AFFOR JAG and paralegals liaise with AOC JAG corps personnel on LOAC and rules of engagement (ROE) issues.

SJA duties to the COMAFFOR include the responsibilities to:

○ Assess the impact of US laws, host-nation laws, and international agreements on the actions and planning of US and coalition forces (e.g., overflight issues, beddown, host-nation support, environmental laws, foreign criminal jurisdiction, legal status of multinational, and US personnel).

○ Assess the impact of international law (especially LOAC) and customary practices, on operations and personnel (e.g., status of civilians, contractors, detainees, and asylum seekers).

○ Provide assessment and guidance on command relationships.

○ Assess the impact of fiscal and contracting authorities on operations.

○ Advise the commander on how to appropriately maintain good order and discipline.

○ Advise the COMAFFOR, AFFOR staff, and subordinate JAG offices on issues involving claims under either US law and directives or applicable international agreements and customary practice (e.g., recompense, claims for property damage, personal injury, or death).

○ Advise the COMAFFOR and subordinate legal offices on the type, nature, and procedural requirements of investigations (e.g., criminal investigations, accident investigations, and friendly fire investigations).

- Advise the COMAFFOR, AFFOR staff, and subordinate JAG offices on general legal issues related to combat support (e.g., ethics, foreign gifts, legal assistance, support to the Army and Air Force Exchange Service).

- Advise the COMAFFOR, AFFOR staff, and subordinate JAG offices on issues regarding civil-military operations.

- Assess law and policy governing domestic use of force and homeland security.

- Assess and advise the COMAFFOR on the availability and applicability of legal authorities and funding to support security cooperation activities with partner nations.

Organization and Manpower

Manning is based upon the expectation of full-time support and advice to the COMAFFOR, AFFOR staff, and subordinate JAG offices. The organization of the COMAFFOR's JAG staff varies based on the scope of the operation and the number of subordinate forces. The COMAFFOR's SJA determines the best way to organize subordinate JAGs and paralegals. A common practice is to organize by subject matter areas (e.g., military justice, international law, fiscal law, civil law, and claims). The SJA is responsible for identifying JAG corps personnel manning requirements for subordinate AFFOR units.

COMAFFOR JAG corps personnel manning should be tailored appropriate to the operation with the goal of minimizing the forward footprint. Reachback and distributed staff capabilities should be considered when determining manning requirements. It also helps to ensure appropriate guidance and oversight is available for subordinate JAGs and paralegals. One known best practice is to select individuals with subject matter expertise in areas such as fiscal law/contracting, international law, military justice, and operational law. The staffing of subordinate units varies based on the mission and size of the subordinate unit being considered. A team of JAGs and paralegals with an appropriate mix of experience and training is desired.[2]

Primary Functions and Capabilities

JAGs and paralegals also contribute their expertise to air component planners in areas of domestic, foreign, and international law that directly affect the conduct of air, space, and cyberspace operations. To meet this challenge, JAGs and paralegals should also have the relevant knowledge, experience, access, and training to function within a joint or multinational environment. Such training might include instruction about the laws governing air and space navigation, the rules governing the use of force, LOAC application, the targeting process, and joint operations planning.

---

[2] For example, an appropriate mix of experience and training may include a combination of fiscal law, contingency contracting, operations law, theater-specific training, accident investigation training, wartime planning, homeland defense, claims, contingency skills training, and the law of war.

INTEGRATION OF LEGAL SUPPORT IN THE AOC

JAGs and paralegals are usually integrated into the various divisions and cells within an AOC. Legal support to an AOC is categorized as a specialty team designed to assist the AOC commander and all AOC divisions. In addition, legal support is provided to assist special functions within a core team such as targeting and rules of engagement cells. As a specialty team, JAGs and paralegals are not directly assigned or dedicated to support a particular division, but are available to support demands from the entire organization.

The COMAFFOR should ensure their JAGs and paralegals are made part of the joint legal staff and the level of legal support meets the requirements of the AOC commander and the JFACC/CFACC if the COMAFFOR is so dual-hatted. The nature and scope of air operations, the operations tempo within the AOC, and the requirements of the supported commander normally determine JAG and paralegal resources given to the AOC.

Legal support in an AOC is provided by JAGs and paralegals with training and security clearances commensurate with their duties. Paralegals assist JAGs in identifying legal issues and supporting functions and processes within an AOC, but **only a JAG may provide legal advice or render a legal opinion**. While the internal organization of an AOC will vary, paralegals provide services to enhance the mission of the AOC, and JAGs provide advice to lawfully achieve mission objectives.

Strategy Division

JAGs and paralegals assist the strategy division by evaluating legal issues raised by the operational environment and the objectives of the supported commander. Within the strategy division, JAGs and paralegals concentrate on long-range planning to support the development, refinement, dissemination, and assessment of the COMAFFOR's plans and operations in support of the JFC's strategy, and the joint air operations plan (JAOP). When supporting the strategy division, JAGs and paralegals focus on long-range planning and execution rather than on the details of day-to-day operations. JAGs and paralegals give tailored legal services to support the planning requirements of the strategy division.

As the JAOP is developed and objectives are identified, JAGs and paralegals review mission objectives found in the strategy and identify legal constraints that may restrict or prevent certain courses of action. JAGs assess the intent of the commander, analyze the proposed course of action in light of the limitations and constraints found in law, policy, or other guidance, and advise the commander on the lawfulness of each course of action. **The primary role of the JAG is to ensure the proposed strategy, including branches and sequels, is consistent with the law, policy, and orders from commanders that govern the operation and to address any legal constraints that may affect joint or coalition forces.**

Combat Plans Division

JAGs and paralegals provide commanders assistance in developing legally acceptable plans and orders that support the JAOP and the guidance issued by the JFC. Within the combat plans division, JAGs facilitate the conversion of strategic guidance into executable plans and orders.

JAGs and paralegals participate in a recurring planning process to assist commanders in identifying, prioritizing, and selecting specific tasks to be accomplished and targets to be engaged with available resources. In this capacity, JAGs advise personnel who produce the following: targeting effects, master air attack plan (MAAP), air tasking order (ATO), and airspace control order (ACO). JAGs and paralegals participate in target list development, production of the MAAP, drafting special instructions, and publishing the ACO and the final daily ATO.

All proposed tactics, targets engaged, and weapons employed are reviewed by JAGs as requested. Their review focuses on operational compliance with international law, domestic law, and applicable national policy. JAGs focus on ensuring tactics, target engagement, and weapons employment are consistent with the LOAC and ROE. For example, a JAG may serve on a joint targeting coordination board or advise a commander on the requirements to protect cultural property and to minimize collateral damage during an air strike. **Although the ultimate decision whether to strike a target rests with the commander, JAGs often review proposed targets and identify legal considerations.**

Combat Operations Division

Within the combat operations division, JAGs and paralegals concentrate on evaluating the legality of employment options designed to support the overall assigned objectives. Accordingly, JAGs provide legal advice concerning personnel recovery operations and attacks on dynamic targets. For example, when attacking dynamic targets, a JAG considers factors including the sufficiency and accuracy of target data, the requirements of the LOAC, compliance with the ROE, and safeguards against fratricide. **Commanders should fully integrate JAGs and paralegals into combat operations processes so that orders will not unnecessarily restrict lawful actions or inadvertently permit unlawful activities.**

JAGs and paralegals should maintain situational awareness to identify legal issues resulting from the execution of planned or time-sensitive operations. JAGs monitor and evaluate tactics, technology, capabilities, or other conditions to identify legal issues that may impact an operation. They recommend commanders modify, or forward a request to modify, the ROE when conditions or circumstances warrant changes to those rules. JAGs and paralegals give advice on the changing nature of operations during execution with the goal of ensuring the legal integrity of military operations. JAGs and paralegals that are properly integrated within the combat operations division are in the best position to understand and identify legal issues that may affect an operation. They remain available to provide immediate legal advice on targets of opportunity and other dynamic operational requirements.

Because of the urgent nature of dynamic targets, JAGs provide critical legal advice immediately. Moreover, JAGs and paralegals should be forward-thinking, anticipating potential legal issues for time-sensitive targets. Commanders should be prepared to seek legal advice if conditions change during air operations. JAGs and paralegals assess targets and form sound legal opinions based on national and other policy, the ROE, and the LOAC to support the commander's objectives.

When potential LOAC violations or instances of fratricide occur, one of two things take place: after mission execution, JAGs and paralegals review battle damage assessment information; and if commander directed, JAG staff initiate or assist in investigations. **If a potential LOAC violation or instance of fratricide has occurred, has been reported, or is suspected, commanders should immediately involve their JAGs and paralegals.** JAGs and paralegals must also report LOAC violations and instances of fratricide through the operational chain of command and take legal action to preserve evidence and information to support future investigations or inquiries.

Air Mobility Division

Within the AMD, JAG corps personnel advise on actions taken to plan, coordinate, task, and execute air mobility operations in support of a larger operation. For example, JAGs may advise the air mobility control team on interpretations of international agreements, risk to ground objects from airdrop, overflight rights, and landing rights.

CHAPTER THREE

JAG CORPS SUPPORT TO AIR FORCE OPERATIONS

> *"The truth of the matter is that you always know the right thing to do. The hard part is doing it."*
>
> **—Norman Schwarzkopf**

This chapter describes how the Air Force JAG Corps conducts legal support to operations. It discusses legal considerations across the range of military operations, operations planning, Air Force legal readiness, mission readiness of JAG Corps personnel, rules of engagement considerations, and rules for the use of force considerations.

JAG CORPS SUPPORT

Air Force JAGs support all Air Force operations. However, some Air Force operations deserve special legal attention including: command and control (C2), air warfare; operations in an irregular warfare (IW) environment; cyberspace operations; air mobility operations; space operations; special operations; homeland operations; information operations (IO); intelligence, surveillance, and reconnaissance (ISR); rescue operations; agile combat support; and Air Reserve considerations.

Command and Control

C2 are not only doctrinal concepts, but are also based on legal requirements and authorities. Command is the lawful authority of the commander derived from the Constitution and from statutes enacted by Congress. Control is the regulation of forces and functions to accomplish the mission in accordance with the commander's intent (including Presidential and Secretary of Defense [SecDef] intent). Combatant commanders (CCDRs) are tasked by law to employ forces. In contrast, Service chiefs are tasked to organize, train, and equip US military forces. As these differing responsibilities require different command relationships and levels of authority, the need to understand legal requirements and authorities becomes increasingly important.

Because command authorities can be expressly created by statute, some agencies have unique command arrangements involving "dual-purpose" forces, such as to the Air Force Intelligence, Surveillance, and Reconnaissance Agency. "Dual-purpose" forces are funded and controlled by organizations that derive authority under laws contained in Title 10 and Title 50, United States Code (U.S.C.). See Appendix E for an explanation of U.S. Code. The greatest benefit of "dual-purpose" forces is their authority to operate under laws contained in Title 50 while being employed by combatant commanders, at the same time, using their Title 10 authority. JAG consultation facilitates operations within dual statutory constructs.

12

Air Warfare

Virtually all aspects of air warfare have legal considerations. Attacks may be restricted by political considerations, military risk, as well as by international law, the LOAC, and ROE. Counterair, strategic attack, counterland, countersea, and personnel recovery operations all are affected by international and host-nation law, particularly the laws governing the sovereignty of a country's land, maritime, and air boundaries. Counter-chemical, biological, radiological, and nuclear operations raise serious implications regarding the lawful use of weapons under the LOAC, as well as US obligations under international arms control treaties. JAG corps personnel have a vital role in training personnel and advising commanders on the legal aspects of targeting. The SJA to the COMAFFOR provides a dedicated legal staff to this practice. JAGs give advice to the warfighter on the legal aspects of targeting.[3]

Operations in an Irregular Warfare Environment

Irregular warfare (IW) is defined as "a violent struggle among state and non-state actors for legitimacy and influence over the relevant populations. IW favors indirect and asymmetric approaches, though it may employ the full range of military and other capacities, in order to erode an adversary's power, influence, and will"[4]. The ROE for activities conducted in an IW environment are often constrained, due to the political and social sensitivities involved when the population, not the military, is the center of gravity. In irregular operations, contingencies can develop rapidly and in non-traditional locations; therefore, long-standing status-of-forces agreements (SOFAs) frequently do not exist. Legal constraints on the use of US funds, equipment, and supplies in support of non-US personnel may be complicated. Other legal challenges may include contingency contracting, the use of non-standard materiel, and the employment of local labor.

Since US strategy is to assist partner nations in building their own security capabilities so they are better able to defend themselves, indirect IW approaches are becoming more widespread. The SJA to the AFFOR plays a critical role in the planning and execution of indirect IW activities by ensuring that the proper legal authorities and funding are available and identified for all security cooperation assistance, both materiel and non-material, provided to partner nations by US forces. If operations progress from indirect support and direct support (not including combat) to direct support (including combat), commanders should anticipate ROE adjustments. In addition, operations conducted in close proximity to civilians may present LOAC and ROE challenges. Commanders should be aware of the potential of rapidly changing ROE and the need to inform subordinates as these changes occur. Understanding commander's intent and ROE can reduce the chances of tactical errors, which can result in strategic setbacks. See AFDD 3-24, *Irregular Warfare*.

---

[3] AFDD 3-0 *Operations and Planning* will expand this concept. It is currently in draft.
[4] JP 1 *Doctrine for the Armed Forces of the United States*

Cyberspace Operations

Domestic and international legal considerations affect virtually every aspect of cyberspace operations. These may involve clarifying who has the authority to conduct what type of operation in cyberspace. It is important to ascertain whether a proposed activity or operation falls within the assigned mission of an Air Force organization. Further, a particular proposed activity or operation may implicate domestic legal issues such as Fourth Amendment rights, statutes designed to protect privacy or those statutes prohibiting misuse of or interference with satellites or other communications systems. Proposed cyberspace operations should also be reviewed for compliance with applicable international law including LOAC. Moreover, some particularly sensitive aspects of operations in cyberspace fall within the purview of the national intelligence community or other interagency members. JAGs should seek additional legal support as necessary by exercising reachback to appropriate headquarters Air Force (HAF) legal offices. See AFDD 3-12, *Cyberspace Operations*.

Air Mobility Operations

Since air mobility operations cover the globe, a broad range of legal issues arise during normal operations. Support from host nations involved in any air mobility operation is essential. Host-nation support is needed to ensure fuel availability for air mobility aircraft. It is paramount to obtain diplomatic clearances from a host nation for both overflight and landing. Past conflicts have demonstrated the ability, or lack thereof, to obtain diplomatic clearances has far-reaching impacts on air mobility efforts. Failure to adequately ascertain host-nation support and provide for any required augmentation can result in mission failure.

JAGs help determine whether a SOFA or other agreements regarding US military presence in the host nation are in effect. If no SOFA or other agreement exists, and legal analysis of the situation/operation proves necessary, proceed in accordance with DOD Directive (DODD) 5530.3, *International Agreements*, and Air Force Instruction (AFI) 51-701, *Negotiating, Concluding, Reporting, and Maintaining International Agreements*, for direction on how to proceed. SOFAs normally include status of personnel, operating rights and responsibilities, possible exemption from landing fees, duties, taxes, boarding/inspection of military aircraft, or personnel entry requirements. Waiver of inspection and boarding of aircraft is essential to maintaining the sovereignty of US military aircraft. Additionally, if agreements are not understood or adhered to by personnel, mission failure is possible. See AFDD 3-17, *Air Mobility Operations*.

Space Operations

The SJA maintains a cadre of JAGs specially trained in air and space law who understand the treaty, policy, and legal considerations associated with space operations. See AFDD 3-14, *Space Operations*.

Special Operations

Planning and execution of special operations may raise legal issues, including LOAC, use of force, fiscal law, environmental law, international agreements, and other legal considerations. The key to avoiding legal obstacles to mission accomplishment is early identification and resolution of potential legal issues before they affect mission success rates. Air Force SOF commanders should ensure qualified legal support is integrated into mission planning, ROE development and publication, aircrew and operator training, and actual mission execution. See AFDD 3-05, *Special Operations*.

Homeland Operations

There are general considerations to legal support regarding homeland operations and the law including financial reimbursement to the DOD.

Any use of DOD assets to collect intelligence on US persons should be in accordance with DODD 5240.1-R, *Procedures Governing the Activities of DOD Intelligence Components that Affect United States Persons*. The *Posse Comitatus Act* (18 U.S.C. §1385) prohibits using members of the Army and Air Force to execute laws in the civilian community, except when authorized by the Constitution or by act of Congress. Congress has passed numerous exceptions to the prohibition. Some examples include the President's ability to invoke the Enforcement of the Laws to Restore Public Order Act (formerly the Insurrection Act), and legislation permitting some use of the military in direct law enforcement roles to counter the influx of illegal narcotics. The exceptions, together with the President's inherent authority under the Constitution, lead to the conclusion that Posse Comitatus does not constitute an insurmountable impediment to the appropriate use of US military resources in support of homeland operations.

When managing the consequences of an event, states normally exercise primacy over domestic incidents. Only when states request federal assistance (or in extraordinary circumstances) does the federal government normally get involved. The request process is a key step for DOD because a formal request by the state followed by Presidential approval is necessary for a military Service to receive financial reimbursement.[5]

Because of legal and policy complexities, prompt and frequent consultations with military legal experts are among the most important considerations in planning for and employing military assets in the homeland environment. See AFDD 3-27, *Homeland Operations*.

Information Operations

There are basic legal considerations that should be taken into account during all aspects of IO planning and execution. JAGs are available at all levels of command in order to assist with these legal considerations. See AFDD 3-13, *Information Operations*.

---

[5] More information can be found in the Stafford Act (42 U.S.C. §§ 5121 *et seq.*).

Intelligence, Surveillance, And Reconnaissance

There are numerous legal issues associated with ISR, especially if ISR operations might impact US persons. ISR activities should be coordinated with JAGs and paralegals to ensure compliance with the law and any existing ROE, as technological advances create numerous legal challenges. Manned and unmanned aircraft will continue to be subject to host-nation overflight and access restrictions in an area of responsibility (AOR). Those limitations are based on international law, custom and practice, and arrangements outlined in the *DOD Foreign Clearance Guide*. See AFDD 2-0, *Global Integrated Intelligence, Surveillance, and Reconnaissance Operations*.

Rescue Operations

JAG personnel provide legal advice to commanders on all aspects of air and ground rescue operations inside and outside the Air Force. Rescue operations consist of a number of specific tasks performed by Air Force units to recover isolated personnel. These operations may be performed in peacetime and wartime throughout the entire spectrum of peaceful and non-peaceful means with a high probability they will be conducted in a joint environment. Due to the quick actions needed to successfully perform rescue operations, JAG personnel familiar with these operations should be readily available to advise commanders and be involved from the beginning of rescue planning activities to the reintegration of recovered personnel. For additional information, see AFDD 3-50, *Personnel Recovery Operations*.

Agile Combat Support

JAG corps personnel provide legal advice to commanders on all areas of combat support to include budget, personnel, military justice, claims, SOFA, international agreements, contracting actions, and specialized support in multinational, civil-military, and combat operations. The JAG provides services that maximize the legal readiness of the force on both organizational and personal levels. See AFDD 4-0, *Agile Combat Support*.

Air Reserve Component (ARC) Considerations

Special considerations exist in determining the command relationships when dealing with the Air National Guard (ANG) and the Air National Guard of the United States (when federalized).[6] The commander exercises command over applicable ANG units and members when they are federalized and in Title 10 status. Administrative control (ADCON) for these federalized units is retained by the ANG Readiness Center. If full mobilization has occurred, command authority is given to the gaining commander. ANG units operating outside of the US or performing federal missions must be in Title 10 status. When ANG personnel are involved in training for a federal mission (Title 32 status), the operational commander may exercise training and readiness oversight, but

---

[6] Because both state Air National Guard and the Air National Guard of the United States relatively go hand-in-hand, they are both usually referred to as just Air National Guard (ANG).

does not possess command authority. In this case, command authority remains with the state authorities. Title 32 status ANG members fall under the command authority of the adjutant general (TAG) of their state, and therefore their governor. If ANG members operate in Title 32 status outside of their state, but within the US, command authority remains with the TAG, but is subject to any coordinating authority or state-to-state agreements. If no pre-negotiated agreement exists, responsibilities such as support and force protection are normally coordinated between applicable commanders.

Similar considerations apply when dealing with the Air Force Reserve (AFR) forces. AFR forces train and operate in a federal status under Title 10. They are similar to ANG forces in being a part-time force, in that they are not continually in an active duty status, but they are subject to the UCMJ when performing official duties. The ARC forces (which by statute include the ANG and the AFR) must be called to active duty as volunteers or involuntarily under specific statutory authority. AFR forces are commanded by the commander of Air Force Reserve Command (AFRC/CC). The AFRC/CC exercises command of AFRC units and members when they are in a military status. ADCON for these federalized units is retained by the AFRC/CC in all locations short of full mobilization. When AFR forces are involved in training, and not actually engaged in combatant commander (CCDR) operations, the operational commander normally exercises training and readiness oversight.[7] All ARC forces are only called to duty for specific periods of time. Care must be taken that their military status is lawfully maintained if it becomes necessary to extend their term of service.

AIR FORCE LEGAL READINESS

Air Force legal readiness is the state of preparation in which Air Force members are ready to deploy, both in their personal and mission capacities. Legal readiness involves awareness of the personal legal issues that may arise in preparation for or during a deployment and the remedies available to avoid or mitigate any adverse effects of those issues. Regarding the mission, legal readiness involves the ability of individuals and their organizations to deal with the legal aspects of the operational environment.

Legal readiness has many facets: pre-deployment targeted legal advice, special and general powers of attorney, will and trust reviews, and general military legal counsel. Appendix A offers the commander additional legal readiness considerations.

MISSION READINESS OF JAG CORPS PERSONNEL

The mission requirements of a location determine legal services needs. To achieve the level of JAG mission readiness needed, SJAs should first determine what is

---

[7] More information about ARC use can be found in the current Global Force Management Implementation Guidance.

required to: support operations controlled, supported, or executed at or from the home station; prepare expeditionary legal support capabilities that are postured within their offices; and prepare to integrate legal support personnel identified to augment their offices. Therefore, the mission readiness of any JAG activity should be evaluated in terms of home station operations, expeditionary legal support, and home station augmentation.

Expeditionary Legal Support

Expeditionary legal support includes the services provided to support forward-deployed forces. Expeditionary legal support consists of the personnel and equipment available to satisfy expeditionary requirements. This requires SJAs to understand their deployment contribution and availability. Expeditionary legal support also includes legal services provided through reachback. Reachback requires that home station resources (e.g., experts in various fields of practice, host-nation advisors, information, equipment) be prepared and available to support forward-deployed forces through the chain of command.

Essential Level of Services and Contingency Mitigation Planning

Each JAG activity determines the essential level of services to fulfill mission requirements by taking mission essential tasks and mandatory performance standards into account. Therefore, SJAs should closely monitor the essential levels of service provided by their activity. They need to plan accordingly for potential changes (possibly caused by deployments or emergencies resulting in minimum manning or minimal resource situations). Forward planning of JAG activities should alleviate possible repercussions and assure full-time mission-essential task accomplishment.

JAG Mission Readiness Preparation

Although not an exhaustive list, JAGs and paralegals may participate in any or all of the following activities to prepare for support operations:

✪ Continuing legal education through civilian, joint, and multinational sources.

✪ Professional education through Air Force, joint, and multinational sources.

✪ Military engagement activities with domestic and foreign agencies and activities.

✪ Comparative law studies and interactions with host-nation legal representatives.

✪ Joint and multinational exercises and training.

✪ Operations planning involvement to direct, control, and sustain Air Force operations.

✪ Evaluation of legal principle application to missions, weapons systems, and tactics.

CONTINGENCY OPERATIONS

JAGs provide decision-makers at all levels with the analysis needed to evaluate options, assess risks, and make law-compliant decisions. During any deployment, Airmen usually face legal issues comparable to those from previous operations. While the topics below are not an exhaustive list, they provide a primer on the types of legal issues addressed by JAG corps personnel in the past. Therefore, JAG personnel remain prepared to address these common legal pitfalls. See Appendix A.

Legal Basis for Mission

The legal basis for a mission aids in defining the parameters, limitations, and scope of the operation. In order for commanders to determine the best course of action to accomplish the mission within the limits set forth by law, they should know the legal basis of the mission. For example, a United Nations (UN) Security Council resolution may provide the legal basis for operating under the UN charter, the authority for the use of force, and the status of participating forces. JAGs assist commanders to focus on the mission, avoid mission creep, and work toward an appropriate end state.

Status of Forces

Commanders should be aware of any legal issues that may adversely affect the mission, including the potential applicability of local, host nation, and international law to Air Force personnel and missions. Determining the status of personnel supporting the military operation is vital. JAGs should ascertain the status of personnel to ensure they understand the rights and obligations in the host nation.

Planning, Coordination, and Oversight

JAG personnel perform a wide variety of planning tasks at the strategic, operational, and tactical levels. They provide legal advice on the myriad regulations, laws, policies, treaties, and agreements that apply to joint military operations. JAG personnel actively participate in the entire planning process from analysis, to course of action (COA) development and recommendation, through execution.

Strategic and operational planning typically occurs at the joint task force (JTF) or at higher echelons. JAG personnel who perform planning tasks at the tactical level typically do so as members at the wing level or below.

JAG participation during operations planning at all levels is vital to mission success. JAGs and paralegals should be integrated into the planning environment and have ready access to needed information and specific personnel who plan and execute the operation. The legal advice provided by JAGs and paralegals is usually mission-specific. For example, supporting a commander who is tasked to provide close air support will have different legal issues than a commander who provides airlift and medical evacuation services. JAG corps personnel provide better legal advice if they understand the organization's mission, weapons, and weapon systems.[8]

Military Justice

Air Force forces should maintain good order and discipline to function effectively and accomplish the mission. JAGs have a duty to ensure advice to commanders is proper so that justice is administered in a fair, consistent, and uniform manner. For example, there cannot be unjustified differences in punishments based on the status of offenders (e.g., officer versus enlisted, regular Air Force versus ANG and AFR). Especially when dealing with ANG and AFR forces, it is important to understand the concurrent military justice authority exercised by both the operational and administrative chains of command and the importance of consultation between commanders when contemplating military justice actions.

Claims

Prompt adjudication and payment of meritorious claims facilitates the mission by providing the host-nation population an avenue to submit claims for loss or damage because of US military operations. JAGs and paralegals are responsible for researching foreign claims procedures and making contact with other military claims activities within country as soon as possible.

Rules for the Use of Force

The appropriate use of force against lawful targets is a primary concern of the commander. JAGs and paralegals should understand the legal aspects of the rule for use of force (RUF) for their operation. JAGs and paralegals should contact their primary ROE/RUF clients—commanders, aircrews, security forces (including augmentees), and SOF personnel to ensure the ROE and RUF facilitate accomplishment of the mission. Commanders should ensure that all personnel receive training in ROE and RUF.

Base Defense

Airmen, particularly security forces personnel, are responsible for detecting and engaging enemy forces that threaten sustained operations. JAG corps personnel should understand the unique legal issues associated with base defense. For example, personnel may be tasked to provide personal protection, escort conveys, or employ crew-served weapons and landmines. JAGs and paralegals should actively engage with Airmen performing base defense duties to ensure they understand the legal issues associated with their actions, ensure the ROE are appropriate for the mission, and investigate and report any potential LOAC violations. Airmen may also be required to operate outside the perimeter of the supported installation to detect potential threats. JAGs and paralegals should be prepared to address legal issues associated with the tactics or weapons that may be used by Airmen performing base defense duties.

---

[8] AFDD 3-0 *Operations and Planning* will expand this concept. It is currently in draft.

Noncombatants and Noncombatant Property

In many cases, JAG corps personnel will be asked to provide legal advice on noncombatant legal issues, LOAC compliance, and LOAC violations. Decisions made concerning noncombatant personnel or property may have a legitimate operational purpose that complies with the LOAC, but JAGs should ensure such actions are properly documented in the event a commander is accused of violating the LOAC.

Contractors and Other Civilians Accompanying the Force

Military operations are increasingly dependent on support from contractors and civilians accompanying the force. JAGs and paralegals should address legal issues associated with the employment of these vital support personnel.

Fiscal and Contracting Issues

Fiscal law is a potentially contentious issue in the deployed environment. Many locations witness increased contracting activity as they seek to expand or enhance their infrastructure and capabilities. Commanders should have a proactive approach, working closely with the JAG, contracting officer, civil engineer, comptroller, and others to ensure that proposed actions remain within the limits of the law. The same basic contracting and fiscal rules (such as the Anti-Deficiency Act[9]) apply in the deployed environment as they do at home station. JAGs, in conjunction with contracting personnel, should assist commanders in ensuring only authorized personnel obligate the government. Special care should be taken to guard unauthorized personnel from entering into contracts and ensure the proper use of funds during the initial stages of a deployment when everyone is focused on "doing what it takes" to complete the mission.

Return of Non-Air Force Property and Facilities

The absence of a large forward-deployed force and our nation's involvement in multiple military operations requires the Air Force to maintain an expeditionary force capable of deploying anywhere in the world at anytime. As a result, the Air Force may need access to property and facilities in support of military operations. At the outset, JAGs should consider what actions are required to return property and facilities back to the owner. Failure to address the liability of US use of private or foreign property and facilities use may result in negative consequences upon return of the property or facilities.

OPERATIONS PLANNING

A COMAFFOR's JAG corps personnel participate in deliberate and crisis action planning by assisting planners in the application of legal considerations and by recommending legally acceptable courses of action to the commander. They are responsible for providing legal advice to decision makers on the myriad of laws, policies,

---

[9] 31 U.S.C., paragraph 1341

treaties, and agreements that influence or impact air, space, and cyberspace operations.

Deliberate Planning

Commanders should seek legal advice during each phase of the deliberate planning process to ensure legal considerations are addressed (see Appendix B). JAGs and paralegals have the following responsibilities during this process:

○ Ensure plans comply with relevant multilateral and bilateral international agreements, international law and domestic law, US government policy, and DOD guidance.

○ Prepare the appropriate appendices and annexes to plans.

○ Review the entire plan with a focus on areas with legal significance (e.g., legal authorities, targeting, fiscal considerations, host-nation support agreements, air navigation, use of force, and status of forces).

○ Review relevant supporting plans to ensure appropriate appendices and legal annexes are complete and provide the necessary guidance.

○ Ensure the amount and type of JAGs and paralegals have been identified to deploy in support of operations, or to support operations in-place.

JAGs and paralegals should be thoroughly familiar with the plans they are tasked to support, the unique legal issues for the supported operational area, and the capabilities of the employment locations they may be tasked to support. The mission of each employment location will uniquely impact legal readiness requirements. Therefore, mission success requires advanced planning by all JAGs and paralegals. See Appendix B, Table B.1. for additional details about the legal support role in deliberate planning.

Crisis Action Planning

The responsibilities of JAGs and paralegals during crisis action planning are similar to those during deliberate planning; however, the time available for legal support planning is compressed. JAGs and paralegals should be familiar with the crisis action planning process and be able to address legal considerations in each phase of the process as outlined in Appendix B, Table B.2.

RULES OF ENGAGEMENT

ROE are rules that govern the use of force to reflect the will of the civilian and military leadership. ROE are defined as "directives issued by competent military authority that delineate the circumstances and limitations under which United States forces will initiate and/or continue combat engagement with other forces encountered"[10]. ROE constrain the actions of forces to ensure their actions are consistent with domestic and international law, national policy, and objectives. ROE

> *The staff judge advocate (SJA) assumes the role of principal assistant to the J-3 [Operations] or J-5 [Plans] in developing and integrating ROE into operational planning.*
>
> **—CJCSI 3121.01,**
> ***Standing Rules of Engagement for US Forces,***
> **Enclosure L**

are based upon domestic and international law, history, strategy, political concerns, and a vast wealth of operational wisdom, experience, and knowledge provided by military commanders and operators. Appendix D offers considerations to assist the commander with ROE development.

Purposes

ROE ensure that any use of force is consistent with national security and policy objectives. Used chiefly to regulate the use of force, ROE either allow or limit the ability and means to employ force. ROE serve political, military, and legal purposes and define the parameters within which Air Force personnel accomplish their missions. They ensure national policy and objectives are reflected in the actions of Air Force forces and set constraints on a commander's actions so they are consistent with domestic and international law and national policy. ROE help ensure the appropriate military capability is applied prudently and often reflect collateral limitations that restrict the use of force far beyond what is required by the LOAC. History has demonstrated that, **to be most effective, ROE should represent a confluence of legal considerations, national**

> *Commanders at all levels are responsible for establishing ROE/RUF for mission accomplishment that comply with ROE/RUF of senior commanders, the Law of Armed Conflict, applicable international and domestic law and this instruction.*
>
> **—Chairman of the Joint Chiefs of Staff Instruction (CJCSI) 3121.01B,** *Standing Rules of Engagement/Standing Rules for the Use of Force for US Forces,* **13 June 2005**

policy objectives, and operational concerns. When the actions of military personnel and units are framed by the disciplined application of force through effective ROE,

---

[10] JP 1-04 *Legal Support to Military Operations*

commanders can make sound judgments and select the best possible course of action to accomplish the mission.

ROE ensure that Air Force forces comply with the LOAC. Although not law, ROE derive much of their influence from the law. Air Force forces adhere to the LOAC and embrace the principles set forth therein, including the principles of military necessity, humanity, proportionality, and discrimination. ROE are an important mechanism to assist commanders in fulfilling their obligations under the LOAC and are often used to reinforce certain principles of the LOAC.

Principles

Absent specific operational necessity, ROE should never impede the inherent right of self-defense of US forces. ROE for US forces should not limit a commander's inherent authority and obligation to use all necessary means available to take action in self-defense of the commander's unit and other US forces in the vicinity. The right and obligation of self-defense should be specified in every set of ROE and should never be compromised; for example, anticipatory self-defense serves as a foundational element in the Chairman of the Joint Chiefs of Staff (CJCS) standing rules of engagement (SROE), in the concept of hostile intent. US forces do not have to be the subject of a hostile act before responding in self-defense. Commanders at every echelon are responsible for establishing or requesting ROE for mission accomplishment that comply with ROE of senior commanders and the SROE.

By following the ROE principles outlined below, Air Force forces' missions have a lesser possibility of being compromised and the chances of US political and military objectives being obtained are increased:

- ✪ **ROE should complement US interests and military objectives.** Commanders should impose restrictions on the use of force when justified to accomplish the mission. Restricting the use of force should be designed in accordance with the commander's intent and mission planning guidance. A proper balance is essential to ensure Air Force forces appropriately respond to enemy forces, as political and diplomatic reasons may exist for controlling the use of force. Commanders should have the latitude and flexibility necessary to employ force to meet military objectives within a broad array of permissible boundaries.

- ✪ **ROE should not be too specific or restrictive.** ROE should restrict the use of force to prevent overreaction or unnecessary escalation of the conflict, but should be permissive enough to ensure friendly forces are not too limited. For example, ROE that are written too broadly may result in an unintentional escalation of conflict or the possibility of fratricide. By contrast, ROE that are too narrow may unnecessarily restrict the effects of Air Force operations.

- ✪ **ROE should be current and responsive to change.** Changing mission requirements equates to a constant review of ROE. ROE should account for changes in political or military objectives, the commander's intent, and the threat to

US forces. For example, ROE that govern information operations should be responsive to changes in the mission, environment, technology, and the evolving threat. Commanders should establish or request changes to the ROE to ensure the use of force is consistent with mission accomplishment and the commander's intent.

○ **ROE should not diminish operational effectiveness.** ROE should permit effective control over forces by the COMAFFOR. ROE should not be specific instructions for how to employ forces, as no set rules—no matter how lengthy or detailed—can address every possible scenario that combat forces may face while conducting operations. ROE should permit flexibility and enable the commander to maximize the contributions of airpower across the spectrum of conflict and support to operations.

○ **ROE should permit the timely and appropriate use of force.** ROE should ensure force is applied in a well-disciplined manner, but should not delay the prompt execution of time-sensitive operations or attacks on targets of opportunity. Commanders should seek clarification or guidance through the chain of command, or submit a request to modify the ROE, if the ROE are not clear or could jeopardize the prompt engagement of time-sensitive targets.

Characteristics

Effective ROE allow commanders to apply the principles of war and the tenets of airpower to support national security objectives without constraining capabilities of forces. To maximize operational effectiveness, ROE should:

○ Be transparent and clearly linked to mission accomplishment.

○ Be continually briefed to all Airmen by commanders, warfighters, and JAGs.

○ Be tailored to the audience and easy to understand, remember, and apply.

○ Be constantly reviewed for modification or amplification.

○ Be simple, clear, brief, and seamless.

○ Avoid excessively qualified language.

○ Avoid mention of strategy or doctrine.

○ Avoid restating the LOAC.

JAG Staff Role in ROE Development

JAGs and paralegals do not own or control the ROE process, but serve as the principal advisor to the COMAFFOR and staff. The JAGs and paralegals have an affirmative duty to provide legal advice to commanders and their staffs that is consistent with the law and the governing ROE at all times. Ordinarily, JAGs provide legal advice to commanders who will select the most appropriate course of action to accomplish the mission. For example, during joint operations, a JAG assists in the development of ROE, but the operators (planning and executing in the operational chain of command) have the responsibility to formulate and submit ROE for approval to the COMAFFOR. In turn, the COMAFFOR presents proposed changes to the JFC.

Developing ROE

JAGs and paralegals provide advice during all levels of operations planning to support and sustain ROE development. They advise commanders and their staffs throughout all phases of the joint operations planning process to help ensure ROE are legally acceptable, operationally feasible, and properly balanced against applicable law, national policy, and commander's intent and guidance. JAGs and paralegals should be involved early in the planning process to ensure effective ROE are developed. Early involvement ensures legal issues are identified and legally acceptable courses of action and supporting ROE are developed consistent with the commander's intent. A thorough understanding of operational issues aids JAGs in preparing advice that allows commanders to achieve their objectives within the limits of the law and national policy. For example, to properly advise an operational commander, a JAG should be fully cognizant of the commander's "no strike" and "restricted" target lists. Involved and engaged JAGs maximize planning efforts and help ensure proper ROE are developed to support mission accomplishment.

ROE should be developed to support the mission requirements of an operation and should be crafted to minimize delays in the execution of time-sensitive operations. For example, during all phases of an operation, from planning to execution, JAGs and paralegals tailor legal advice to support the targeting cycle. JAGs assist in the development of ROE that allow Air Force forces to attack time-sensitive targets effectively.

ROE development and mission planning are collaborative processes and require significant staff integration. ROE development is best achieved when legal support and operators collaborate to develop ROE or request supplemental measures to fully implement the commander's intent. JAGs advise operations and planning staffs on the legality of proposed ROE and, when necessary, recommend actions to ensure compliance with the law and policy.

Interpreting ROE

An Air Force JAG's ROE role is that of an interpreter and advisor, not a decision maker. JAGs and paralegals interpret ROE to support the execution of time-sensitive operations. Legal staff should understand the intent of the President, SecDef, CCDR, and subordinate commanders when preparing advice on ROE. A JAG's primary duty is accurate counsel to command on the law and the commander's responsibilities with respect to the law. In this advisory capacity, JAGs focus on interpreting the ROE, the

LOAC, and other guidance to develop legal recommendations that will advance the commander's objectives. Thus, JAGs should be thoroughly familiar with international and domestic law, national policy, operations orders, and other information to interpret intent and meaning of ROE, effectively. After considering legal advice, commanders ultimately exercise their discretion, wisdom, and decision-making authority to select the best course of action that will comply with the law and further mission accomplishment.

JAGs and paralegals interpret ROE issued from multiple sources. Each operation has a unique set of ROE to support the needs of a particular mission. Generally, combatant commanders and higher authority establish ROE. ROE usually incorporates political, military, and legal concerns. For all US operations, the CJCS SROE is the starting point for ROE unless rules have been previously established in contingency plans or through agreements with other nations. Drafting ROE to support multinational forces under the operational control of a US or a foreign commander requires detailed coordination and a thorough understanding of the laws, policies, and political objectives of each contributing nation. JAGs and paralegals develop comparative law studies that identify the legal requirements of each nation to ensure multinational ROE will not conflict with the obligations of each contributing nation. JAGs support commanders by analytically interpreting legal requirements and obligations of other nations. They also deduce ROE from multiple sources.

Modifying ROE

JAGs and paralegals assist commanders in modifying or requesting changes to the ROE. With few exceptions, ROE are fundamentally permissive in nature and allow commanders to modify or request changes to the ROE to support mission accomplishment. At various levels in the operational chain of command, ROE supplemental measures may be approved to allow or limit the use of force for mission accomplishment. JAGs and paralegals assist commanders in determining appropriate ROE and recommend changes when necessary. Commanders should seek modification to ROE through the chain of command. Modification and clarification may be warranted when the ROE are inadequate, faulty, create the risk of fratricide, or hinder a commander's ability to carry out the mission.

Implementing ROE

Air Force commanders expect JAGs to know and fully advise Air Force forces on ROE. JAGs and paralegals at every stage of an operation maintain situational awareness of current ROE and should be prepared to recommend changes to the commander.

JAGs and paralegals assist commanders in fulfilling their obligations to implement and disseminate ROE. In addition, they work in concert with commanders and their staffs to train forces on the ROE and to standardize and interpret their intent and meaning. JAGs provide tailored ROE training to various audiences, from aircrews to security forces. For example, JAGs may provide training on ROE, status of personnel, mission and forces, Code of Conduct for US Forces, and other constraints imposed by the law.

RULES FOR THE USE OF FORCE

JAGs advise commanders on the RUF that apply when DOD forces are performing civil support missions and routine Service functions including force protection within the US and its territories or when DOD forces are performing law enforcement or security duties within (when permitted by Posse Comitatus) or outside the US. JAG corps personnel advise commanders on the process for seeking RUF modification, as required. JAG corps personnel also train Service members on the RUF or RUF policies for law enforcement and security operations.

CONCLUSION

This doctrine document described the power of command, including fundamental legal aspects, legal roles and responsibilities of the COMAFFOR, and common legal issues. Commanders at all levels and across the range of military operations (ROMO) should be familiar with JAG roles and capabilities. Legal and operational readiness of the force is critical. JAGs support Air Force operations at all levels by providing Air Force commanders the legal analysis and advice needed to make informed and legally sound decisions. Whether JAG corps personnel are tasked to support humanitarian operations or combat operations during a major theater war, JAG corps personnel remain prepared.

Because Air Force missions are demanding, precise, and many times are performed in Air Force expeditionary operations and complex international environments , the very best in legal capability is essential for mission success. The Air Force JAG Corps supplies a talented and highly trained group of military legal professionals—attorneys and paralegals, civilian, Active Duty regular Air Force, Air National Guard, and Reserve members. These members ensure the JAG Corps is capable of providing mission essential full-time legal support to our Air Force, both today and in the future.

APPENDIX A

LEGAL CONSIDERATIONS IN AIR FORCE OPERATIONS

Legal Basis for Mission

Upon deployment, commanders and JAGs should be prepared to address the following questions concerning the legal basis for an operation:

✪ What is the mission (e.g., peacekeeping, peace enforcement, humanitarian assistance/disaster relief, armed conflict)?

✪ Is this a UN, allied, coalition, or US only operation? How does this support effect operations (e.g., treaty obligations, political issues, and cultural sensitivities)?

✪ Has the use of force been authorized (e.g., "all necessary means")?

✪ What is the funding authority for this operation?

✪ What is the chain of command? Are US forces participating in a multinational operation under the operational control of a US commander?

Status of Forces

Upon deployment, commanders and JAGs should be prepared to address the following questions concerning the legal status of forces operating in a host nation:

✪ What is the status of US forces in the host nation (e.g., SOFA, UN expert on mission)?

✪ How might this status affect the operation? Are there any restrictions on carrying weapons?

✪ Who does the COMAFFOR contact if host-nation authorities detain a US Service member?

✪ What is the status of the different types of civilians accompanying the force in the host nation?

✪ What is the US obligation concerning airport/landing fees, taxes, duties, entrance requirements?

Use of Force

When deploying, JAGs should address the following legal issues concerning the use of force:

✪ What are the ROE and RUF?

- When and what do US forces engage?

- What weapons or weapon systems can be used to destroy/neutralize any given target? Who is the release authority for each weapon or weapon system?

- Who does a COMAFFOR contact to adjust the ROE or RUF, and how?

- Have personnel received LOAC training? Do they understand the concepts and elements of individual self-defense, unit self-defense, national self-defense, and collective self-defense?

- Can US forces provide training to others who provide external protection or security services (e.g., foreign forces, local or host-nation police, contractors, NGO employees)?

- Can US forces perform "law enforcement" functions (e.g., stop civilian-on-civilian violence, detain civilians, search, or seize civilian property)?

Planning, Coordination, and Oversight

In operations planning, there are a number of basic legal issues to be addressed:

- Who are our allies? Who are the combatants?

- What is the "operational interpretation" of the ROE (e.g., hostile intent, hostile act)?

- What is the status of a pilot, aircrew, or aircraft if it is shot down or forced to land?

- Where can US aircraft fly without obtaining clearance (e.g., international airspace, overflight of excessive territorial claims)?

- What actions does a COMAFFOR take if a foreign nation wants to inspect, search, or decontaminate US aircraft?

- Are there any unique legal issues associated with the weapons or weapons systems present at any given location deployment location?

Military Justice

Some issues to be addressed to ensure an effective military justice system include:

- Who are the court-martial convening authorities? What are the command relationships?

- What offenses does the US have primary jurisdiction over? Host nation?

- How does a COMAFFOR handle "joint justice" issues? Who is the senior Air Force officer?

✪ What control measures are or should be imposed (e.g., US Central Command General Order #1)?

✪ What arrangements have been made for defense services?

✪ Will courts-martial be conducted at the operating location? If not, where?

✪ How are Airmen made aware of commander directives (such as General Order #1 above)? Do members understand the contents of the commander's directives?

✪ What constitutes a "serious incident" at the operating location?

✪ Are all commanders on G-series orders?

✪ Who can discipline Guard and Reserve personnel? Can they be extended at the operating location to complete disciplinary actions?

Claims

There are certain questions about claims that should be asked in any operation:

✪ Who has claims jurisdiction under DOD Directive 5515.9, *Single-Service Assignment of Responsibility for Claims Processing*?

✪ Has a foreign claims commission been appointed?

✪ What do applicable international agreements say about claims liability and processing?

✪ Where will a claims office be set up to receive and process claims from host-nation personnel?

✪ Who will investigate claims? How will they travel?

✪ Are there any unique tort provisions in the host-nation law? Is there a comparative law study?

✪ How are claims processed under the SOFA or other international agreements?

✪ Are solatium payments authorized (e.g., Korea or Japan)?

Fiscal and Contracting Issues

When deploying, JAGs should address the following legal issues concerning fiscal and contracting actions:

✪ Who is authorized to obligate the government (i.e., who has a contracting warrant)?

✪ What funds are available to set up and sustain the operation? Who is keeping track of what is purchased and for how much?

✪ What are the sources and methods available for acquisition of goods and services?

✪ What do applicable international agreements say about building or repairing items in the host nation?

✪ Do contracts include claims provisions? What is the US obligation under the provision?

✪ What support can US forces provide foreign armed forces? Is there an acquisition and cross-servicing agreement between the US and other foreign forces?

Base Defense

When deploying, JAGs should address the following legal issues concerning Airmen performing base defense duties:

✪ Who is performing the base defense duties? Are these Air Force security forces personnel? Are these augmentees? What authority and responsibilities does the commander have for directing base defense?

✪ What weapons do Airmen have at the deployed location and what are legal issues regarding the use of such weapons (e.g., mortars, hollow-point ammunition, incendiaries)?

✪ Do Airmen understand the ROE? Do they understand the concepts and elements of "individual self-defense," "unit self-defense," "national self-defense," and "collective self-defense?"

✪ Has "mission essential property" been designated? If not, should it be designated?

✪ What are the legal issues associated with the use of riot control agents, other non-lethal weapons, and landmines?

✪ Do Airmen understand the procedures for searching and seizing property? What are the legal issues and procedures regarding searching and seizing host-nation property?

✪ What should Airmen do if they witness civilian-on-civilian violence?

✪ Is there a plan for handling enemy prisoners of war, civilian detainees, or those seeking temporary refuge? Has a detention facility been established? Is it properly marked? How and when does the Air Force transfer detainees to others (e.g., other US forces [typically Army] or the host nation)?

✪ Do Airmen understand how to treat host-nation civilians? Can Airmen detain them? For what? How? How long? What do Airmen do with them once they get them? What if the host nation is unable or unwilling to prosecute or control them?

✪ What are the legal issues associated with using ISR to support operations in the different operating environments: CONUS; OCONUS hosted; and expeditionary?

Noncombatants and Noncombatant Property

When supporting combat operations, JAGs should address the following legal issues concerning noncombatants:

✪ Have medical personnel and chaplains been properly identified and do they exclusively perform noncombatant duties?

✪ Are noncombatant facilities, equipment, and vehicles being used to support combatant activities?

✪ Are noncombatant facilities, aircraft, vehicles, equipment, and supplies properly marked? If not, has an operational purpose been identified to preclude such marking?

✪ Have medical facilities been located away from military objectives such as command and control facilities and supply staging areas? If not, has an operational purpose been identified to justify the current location?

✪ Do medical personnel prioritize medical treatment based on military status, occupation, rank, or nationality or do they use triage (i.e., screening of patients to determine priority medical needs) to assist the wounded, sick, or injured in a methodical manner?

Contractors and Other Civilians Accompanying the Force

When deploying, JAGs should address the following legal issues concerning contractors and civilians accompanying the force:

✪ What is their status?

✪ Who is responsible for protecting them? Can they be armed for their own self-defense?

✪ Do they participate in combatant activities?

✪ Does a commander have to provide protective equipment (e.g., chemical warfare) and training? What can or cannot the commander provide (e.g., food, transportation, shelter, medical care)?

✪ What, if any, disciplinary authority does a commander have over them? What happens if they are unable or unwilling to satisfy their obligations under the contract?

Redeployment Activities

When redeploying, JAGs should address the following legal issues concerning property or facilities:

✪ What environmental laws will apply?

✪ What is the US liability concerning the property?

✪ What is the condition of the property?

✪ May the US make improvements to the property? Temporary or permanent?

✪ How will the US dispose of or transfer the temporary improvements or facilities?

✪ What controls are in place to ensure US property is properly disposed of (e.g., returned to the US, transferred to the Defense Reutilization and Marketing Office, abandoned)?

✪ Are host-nation claims of damage being properly analyzed in light of US law and applicable international agreements?

✪ What is the disposition of property purchased at the deployment location (e.g., televisions, fitness equipment)? Who has accounted for it?

✪ What will happen to "minor military construction" projects (e.g., tent platforms, guard shacks)?

APPENDIX B

DELIBERATE AND CRISIS ACTION PLANNING

Table B.1. Legal Support Role in Deliberate Planning.[11]

Deliberate Planning	
Combatant Commander	**Role of Legal Support**
Phase I – Strategic Guidance / Joint Strategic Capabilities Plan Initiation	
Assign planning tasks to supported combatant commanders.	Review planning documents.
Specify the types of plans required. Apportion forces and resources.	Review applicable laws, policies, treaties, and Agreements.
Issue planning guidance.	
Phase II – Concept Development	
Review and approve the supported combatant commander's strategic concept.	Review the combatant commander's strategic concept for compliance with law and policy and make appropriate recommendations.
The product: A concept of operations (CONOP)	Coordinate legal issues with counterparts.
Phase III – Plan Development	
Assist the supported combatant commander.	Assist the supported combatant command staff judge advocate.
The product: A complete OPLAN	
Phase IV – Plan Review	
In coordination with the Joint Chiefs of Staff, Services, and Department of Defense agencies, assess and validate the supported combatant commander's operation plan (OPLAN) and time-phased force and deployment data using criteria of adequacy, feasibility, acceptability, and compliance with joint doctrine.	Review the supported combatant command's OPLAN for legal sufficiency and make appropriate recommendations.
Approve or disapprove the OPLAN for reasons stated.	Coordinate legal issues with counterparts.
Identify specific actions planned or programmed to redress any shortfalls.	
The product: An approved OPLAN	
Phase V – Supporting Plans	
Resolve critical issues that arise during the supported combatant command's review of supporting plan.	Crosswalk supporting plans to ensure they are legally correct, complete, and consistent, and make appropriate recommendations.

---

[11] Derived from JP 1-04, *Legal Support to Joint Operations Planning*

Table B.2. Legal Support Role in Crisis Action Planning. [12]

Crisis Action Planning		
Supported Combatant Commander	**Supported Combatant Commander's Staff Judge Advocate (SJA)**	**Air Force Component SJA**
Phase I – Situation Awareness		
Detailed plan development. Issue guidance to subordinate and supporting commanders. Situation Development. Detect, report, and assess events that have potential national security implications to determine whether a military response may be required. Report actions being taken, forces available, expected time for earliest commitment of forces, and major constraints on the employment of forces.	Situation Development. Contact legal counterparts and establish the basis for concurrent planning. Review planning documents. Review applicable laws, policies, treaties, agreements, and arrangements in all affected AORs. Summarize relevant legal considerations (authorities, restraints, and constraints) and provide them to the crisis action team, combatant commanders, and counterparts. Crisis assessment. Refine the legal considerations.	Review planning documents. Research applicable laws, policies, treaties, and agreements. Summarize relevant legal considerations (authorities, restraints, and constraints) and provide them to the crisis action team, combatant commander, and counterparts.

---

[12] See JP 1-04, *Legal Support to Joint Operations Planning*

Crisis Action Planning		
Supported Combatant Commander	**Supported Combatant Commander's Staff Judge Advocate (SJA)**	**Air Force Component SJA**
Phase II – Planning		
COA Development. In coordination with subordinate and supporting commanders, develop and analyze COAs. Review and use applicable plans. Issue guidance to subordinate and supporting commanders. Submit the commander's estimate to the President and/or SecDef and Chairman of the Joint Chiefs of Staff. Begin detailed execution planning upon receipt of a planning order or alert order.	Incorporate legal considerations and instructions for developing ROE and RUF in the combatant commander's planning guidance. Review the combatant commander's estimate for compliance with law and policy and make appropriate recommendations. Coordinate legal issues and support requirements with counterparts. Contact legal counterparts and facilitate concurrent planning. Review and validate any JAG JTF joint manning document requirements and synchronize joint legal support. Participate in boards, cells and working groups, as required.	Assess legal implications of developments. Discuss rules of engagement needs with commander and counterparts. Coordinate legal issues and support requirements with counterparts. Encourage forces to prepare wills and powers of attorney and resolve legal matters prior to mobilization.
Phase III – Execution		
Execute the operation order. Report force shortfalls to CJCS for resolution.	Monitor operations for legal issues as required. Ensure legal arrangements for deployment/redeployment with host-nations are in place through US Embassies on all affected AORs.	Brief commanders and forces on legal environment.

APPENDIX C

LEGAL READINESS CONSIDERATIONS

Readying the Force

While not an exhaustive list, JAGs and paralegals may take any or all of the following actions to ready the force:

○ Advise commanders of forces preparing for deployment.

○ Develop and implement robust preventive law programs.

○ Participate in the logistics support process to obtain, pre-position, or transfer resources to sustain operations.

○ Provide training and mission-related legal assistance on the legal issues influencing readiness (e.g., estate planning, LOAC, ROE).

○ Prepare legal support capabilities for deployment.

Preparing the Operational Environment

Following are examples of the actions JAGs and paralegals may take to prepare the force:

○ Identify and resolve legal issues within the operational environment (e.g., host-nation support, use of force, environmental constraints).

○ Remove, document, or resolve legal impediments encountered during base support planning activities.

○ Determine legal reachback capabilities and requirements available to support forward deployed forces and those required to sustain operations.

○ Identify legal support requirements and capabilities needed to support operations (e.g., legal services, equipment, facilities).

Positioning the Force

JAGs and paralegals may take any or all of the following actions to position the force:

○ Deploy as part of advance and reception teams or operational cadre to receive and beddown deploying forces.

○ Participate in negotiations for host-nation support and the status of US forces in a host-nation (e.g., foreign criminal jurisdiction, landing fees, use of facilities, claims provisions, taxes).

- Develop comparative law studies of the operational environment (e.g., civil and criminal procedures, summary of unique host-nation laws, rights of US personnel apprehended by host-nation authorities).

- Support logistics processes to obtain goods and services from the local economy (e.g., contingency contracting actions, environmental law, and land use issues).

- Assist commanders and their staffs in developing local policies and procedures to protect the force and maintain discipline (e.g., General Order #1; Force Protection Plan).

- Educate deploying forces on legal issues and policies that apply to the location and operations conducted from the location (e.g., host-nation law, ROE, claims provisions).

- Liaison with applicable US agencies and nongovernmental organizations within the host-nation.

Employing the Force

Following are some examples of actions JAGs and paralegals may take to employ the force:

- Refine the legal support requirements for the location and establish reachback connectivity.

- Accomplish mission training for the supported population (e.g., ROE, LOAC, General Order #1).

- Support actions to generate operational elements of the force (e.g., logistics support, operations planning, target reviews).

- Develop and organize legal services to support continuing operations (e.g., legal assistance, claims services, military justice support, and legal support to C2).

Sustaining the Force

While not an exhaustive list, JAGs and paralegals may take any or all of the following actions to sustain the force:

- Provide full-spectrum legal services to Air Force forces at forward operating locations (e.g., courts-martial, legal assistance, claims, C2 support).

- Employ legal reachback capabilities to enhance legal services (e.g., connectivity to legal information services, liaison with legal specialists).

- Refine legal support requirements and adjust legal services to meet mission requirements (e.g., ROE changes, tax program, and upgraded equipment).

- Provide continuous support for the logistics processes (e.g., military construction, long-term service contracts, and new contracts).

- Support C2 activities and ongoing operations (e.g., ROE training, target reviews, ATO generation).

Recovering the Force

Examples of actions JAGs and paralegals may take to recover the force:

- Address legal issues concerning real property, materials, and real estate that are returned to the owner or host-nation (e.g., environmental impact, value of improvements to facilities).

- Provide mission-related personal legal services to recovering Air Force forces.

- Ensure defense goods and services are sold, transferred, disposed of, or returned in accordance with law and policy (e.g., fitness equipment, temporary facilities, tent platforms, supplies).

- Adjudicate and settle claims for and against US forces (e.g., personal injury, property damage).

- Provide legal support to forces remaining behind to support recovery operations (e.g., legal assistance, contracting support, and logistics).

- Consider whether the limited time ARC forces are called to duty drive any special redeployment prioritization or processing.

APPENDIX D

ROE CONSIDERATIONS

What do the ROE say?

- When can US forces and others be defended?

- What can be attacked?

- How can it be attacked?

- Where can it be attacked?

- When can it be attacked?

- Whose permission is needed to attack?

What purpose do the ROE serve?

- Provide guidance on the use of force—political, military, and legal.

- Control the transition from peace to war (or vice versa).

- Provide a mechanism to facilitate planning.

- Prevent fratricide, civilian casualties, national/coalition political damage, or mission failure.

Have ROE been agreed upon for multinational operations?

- By military commanders?

- By policy makers?

- Do the ROE of the multinational force permit the same degree of individual self-defense and unit self-defense as the US SROE?

ROE Fundamentals

Mission Planning

- ROE are not a substitute for guidance, intent, and judgment or planning.

- ROE development is a collaborative process involving commanders, operators, JAGs, and others.

- ✪ ROE development is an integral part of operations planning including branch/sequel plans.

- ✪ ROE development begins with mission analysis.

- ✪ ROE instructions are set out in the commander's initial planning guidance.

- ✪ ROE development is tied to COA development.

- ✪ COA analysis includes ROE refinement.

Advisories

- ✪ US ROE are fundamentally permissive.

- ✪ Brief current ROE at every JTF update.

- ✪ Monitor ROE training and interpretation.

- ✪ Do not substitute ROE for planning.

- ✪ Use serial ROE messages and not appendices.

- ✪ Do not just ask for ROE—justify ROE.

- ✪ Resolve ROE disputes **before** the fight.

- ✪ Understand that ROE during irregular warfare are normally more restrictive than in traditional war.

ROE Game Plan

Establish a close working relationship with your JAG.

- ✪ Early judge advocate involvement in each of the AOC divisions helps satisfy the legal review obligations under the LOAC and avoids potential last-minute problems with ATO approval and mission execution.

- ✪ JAGs can identify and defuse potential showstoppers with host nations and overflight early in the planning process.

- ✪ JAGs can assist operators in getting clear, concise ROE and special instructions crafted and approved.

Establish an ROE cell to enhance mission planning and execution. A critical function is JAG involvement at inception to maximize planning efforts and to yield lawful ROE.

- ✪ Formulate ROE requests based on JFC objectives, guidance, and intent.

✪ Ensure adequate dissemination of:

    ✪ ✪ Chairman of the CJCS SROE.

    ✪ ✪ Any theater-specific ROE.

    ✪ ✪ Mission-specific ROE (often termed "serial ROE").

    ✪ ✪ Applicable multinational or coalition ROE.

✪ Determine if ROE amendments/supplements are needed.

✪ Institute scenario-based ROE training (JAGs can coordinate efforts).

Determine the effect of the ROE. ROE and international law, to include LOAC, often impact targeting decisions. A good rule of thumb is to factor these restraints into the planning/targeting process early on.

Establish combat identification procedures that are consistent with the ROE.

✪ Allow units and individuals to conduct actions appropriate for self-defense.

✪ Adjust ROE to fit warfighter needs.

APPENDIX E

OVERVIEW OF US CODE SECTIONS IMPACTING DOD

United States Codes (U.S.C.) – Federal law is codified and compiled in the US Code, which is comprised of 50 different titles that generally deal with different areas of the law. An overview of the different U.S. Code titles that impact DOD operations follows:

Title 10 – Armed Forces
- Title 10 has five subtitles: General Military Law; Army; Navy and Marine Corps; Air Force; and Reserve Components.

- Title 10 generally includes federal law that impacts the Department of Defense, the various individual military departments, the Joint Chiefs of Staff, and all manner of military issues.

- When discussing regular and reserve component forces, regular component forces are sometimes referred to as "Title 10" forces.

Title 18 – Crimes and Criminal Procedure
- Title 18 addresses federal crimes and criminal procedure.

- Crimes alleged to have been committed by US military personnel are primarily addressed through the Uniform Code of Military Justice, which is addressed in Title 10.

Title 32 – National Guard
- Title 32 has five subchapters addressing: Organization; Personnel; Training; Service, Supply and Procurement; and Homeland Defense Activities.

- Title 32 generally addresses the federal operations of the National Guard.

- When acting in a state capacity under Title 32, or on State active duty status, then state law is also applicable.

- When discussing active and reserve component forces, National Guard forces are sometimes referred to as "Title 32" forces when they are acting in their state capacity.

Title 50 – War and National Defense
- Title 50 generally addresses intelligence and surveillance activities by US government agencies and other issues relating to war, insurrection and national defense.

REFERENCES

Air Force Publications

All AFDDs are available at https://wwwmil.maxwell.af.mil/au/lemay/main.asp .

All AFDDs, both draft and approved, are also available at the LeMay Center doctrine Community of Practice at:
 https://afkm.wpafb.af.mil/ASPs/CoP/OpenCoP.asp?Filter=OO-OP-AF-44

Air Force Judge Advocate General's Corps (WebFLITE): https://aflsa.jag.af.mil/cgi-bin/thome.cgi

Joint Publications

Note: All JPs are available at : https://jdeis.js.mil/jdeis/index.jsp

Other Publications

Department of the Air Force, *Air Force Operations and the Law—A Guide for Air and Space Forces* (The Judge Advocate General's School Publication) 2009. Available electronically at http://www.afjag.af.mil/library/

Department of the Air Force, *Military Commander and the Law* (The Judge Advocate General's School Publication), 2010. Available electronically at http://www.afjag.af.mil/library/

Zinni, Anthony C., Lt Gen, USMC, *The SJA in Future Operations*, (Marine Corps Gazette), 1996.

Chief of Staff of the Air Force (CSAF) Professional Reading Program

The CSAF's professional reading list, with links to book reviews, is available on the Air Force web site at: http://www.af.mil/library/csafreading/. The list is subject to revision. Readers are encouraged to check the Air Force web site (http://www.af.mil) for the most current information.

GLOSSARY

Abbreviations and Acronyms

ACO	airspace control order
ADCON	administrative control
AETF	air expeditionary task force
ARC	air reserve component
AFDD	Air Force Doctrine Document
AFFOR	Air Force forces
AFLOA	Air Force Legal Operations Agency
AFR	Air Force Reserve
AMC	Air Mobility Command
AMD	air mobility division
AOC	air operations center
ATO	air tasking order
C2	command and control
CCDR	combatant commander
CJCS	Chairman, Joint Chiefs of Staff
COA	course of action
COMAFFOR	commander, Air Force forces
FSC	field support center
IO	information operations
ISR	intelligence, surveillance and reconnaissance
IW	irregular warfare
JA	judge advocate
JAG	judge advocate general
JAOP	joint air operations plan
JFACC	joint force air component commander
JFC	joint force commander
JP	joint publication
LOAC	law of armed conflict
MAAP	master air attack plan
NAF	numbered Air Force
OPCON	operational control
OPLAN	operation plan
OPORD	operation order

ROE	rules of engagement
RUF	rules for use of force
SECAF	Secretary of the Air Force
SecDef	Secretary of Defense
SJA	staff judge advocate
SOF	special operations forces
SOFA	status of forces agreements
SROE	standing rules of engagement
TAG	The Adjutant General
TJAG	The Judge Advocate General of the Air Force
U.S.C.	United States Code
UN	United Nations

Definitions

host nation. A nation which receives the forces and/or supplies of allied nations and/or NATO organizations to be located on, to operate in, or to transit through its territory. (JP 3-57)

host-nation support. Civil and/or military assistance rendered by a nation to foreign forces within its territory during peacetime, crises or emergencies, or war based on agreements mutually concluded between nations. Also called **HNS.** (JP 4-0)

irregular warfare. A violent struggle among state and non-state actors for legitimacy and influence over the relevant population(s). (JP 1)

judge advocate. An officer of the Judge Advocate General's Corps of the Army, Air Force, Navy, Marine Corps, and the United States Coast Guard who is designated as a judge advocate. Also called **JA.** (JP 1-04)

law of war. That part of international law that regulates the conduct of armed hostilities. Also called **the law of armed conflict.** See also **rules of engagement.** (JP 1-04)

reachback. The process of obtaining products, services, applications, forces, equipment, or materiel from organizations that are not forward deployed. (JP 3-30)

rules of engagement. Directives issued by competent military authority that delineate the circumstances and limitations under which United States forces will initiate and/or continue combat engagement with other forces encountered. Also called **ROE.** (JP 1–04)

staff judge advocate. A judge advocate so designated in the Army, Air Force, or Marine Corps, and the principal legal advisor of a Navy, Coast Guard, or joint force command who is a judge advocate. Also called **SJA.** (JP 1-04)

status of forces agreement. An agreement that defines the legal position of a visiting military force deployed in the territory of a friendly state. (JP 3-16)

standing rules of engagement. Fundamental policies and procedures governing the actions to be taken by US commanders and their forces during all military operations and contingencies and routine Military Department functions occurring outside US territory and outside US territorial seas. They provide implementation guidance on the application of force for mission accomplishment and the exercise of self-defense. Also called **SROE.** (CJCSI 3121.01B)

www.ingramcontent.com/pod-product-compliance
Lightning Source LLC
Chambersburg PA
CBHW080550290526
45790CB00006B/2616